# THE DAREDEVIL'S GUIDE

# TO OUTER SPACE

Anna Brett and Mike Jacobsen

# CONTENTS

ACKNOWLEDGEMENTS

| | |
|---|---|
| Publishing Director | Piers Pickard |
| Publisher | Hanna Otero |
| Commissioning Editor | Joe Fullman |
| Author | Anna Brett |
| Illustrator | Mike Jacobsen |
| Consultant | Dr Mike Goldsmith |
| Art Director | Andy Mansfield |
| Print Production | Lisa Ford |

Published in May 2019 by Lonely Planet Global Limited
CRN: 554153
ISBN: 978 1 78868 258 9
www.lonelyplanetkids.com
© Lonely Planet 2019

10 9 8 7 6 5 4 3 2 1

Printed in Singapore

# MISSION STATUS

Astronauts Eddie and Junko, your mission, if you choose to accept it, is to explore our **Solar System**... and beyond. It's an adventure that no human has attempted before!

Mission accepted! A little danger never scared me.

You better get your suit on Eddie, we're blasting off next!

Helmet

Radio Headset

Drinking Tube

Multi-function arms

Multi-layered suit

Thick boots and heated gloves

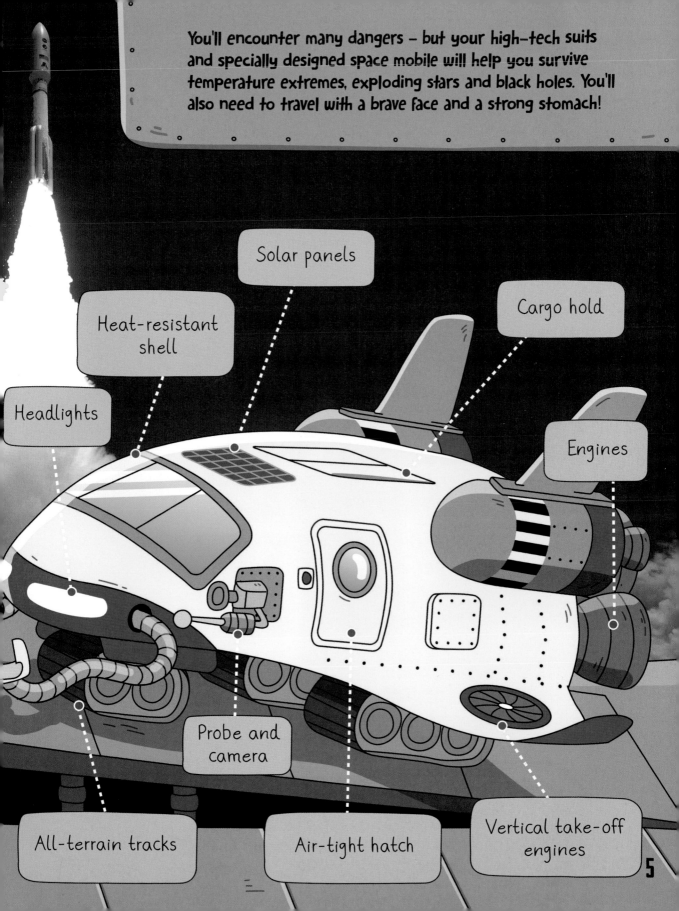

Our mission is divided into three sections. If we were to travel at the speed of light, it would take us 300 million years to reach the furthest stop on the journey! But luckily the space mobile can travel at warp speed, so we should be back in time for our next birthdays.

**PART 1: ABOVE EARTH**
To reach outer space, we first have to fly through Earth's atmosphere and avoid a collision with all the satellites, telescopes and space stations orbiting the planet.

**PART 2: THE SOLAR SYSTEM**
The second section of the journey will take us on a tour of our Solar System. The system consists of one star (our Sun), eight planets, multiple moons and millions of asteroids.

**PART 3: THE MILKY WAY AND BEYOND**
Once we leave the Solar System, we'll see wonders such as newborn stars, **supernova** explosions and glittering **galaxies**. However, we will also have to avoid deadly black holes if we want to make it home again.

# BLAST OFF!

three, two, one... lift-off! Goodbye Earth and hello adventure! There are many dangers associated with launching the space mobile. For starters, in order to push through Earth's atmosphere and escape the pull of **gravity**, we need to move at an extremely rapid 40,000 kph (25,000 mph) – this is known as the 'escape velocity'. But with all this rocket fuel and burning flames, it's like we're sitting on a bomb – thankfully, this is one of the safest spaceships ever built!

This is one of the most dangerous parts of the trip!

The thrust pushing the space mobile up has to be greater than its weight and the drag of air resistance.

What did you say, Junko? The noise from this blast off is double the maximum threshold for human ears. Good job we're wearing our ear plugs.

When accelerating so quickly, it's as if gravity increases up to three times. We feel this as increased weight, known as G-force, pushing us into our seats. If the G-force gets too much, it can stop **oxygen** flowing to the brain, resulting in unconsciousness. So we have to stay alert!

## LAUNCH STATS

**LAUNCH LOCATION:** KENNEDY SPACE CENTER, USA, EARTH

**COST OF LAUNCH:** US$450 MILLION

**ESCAPE VELOCITY:** 40,000 KPH (25,000 MPH)

**FIRST OBJECT IN SPACE:** V-2 ROCKET MW18014, 1944, GERMANY

**FIRST CREATURE IN SPACE:** LAIKA THE DOG, 1957, SOVIET UNION

**FIRST HUMAN IN SPACE:** YURI GAGARIN ABOARD *VOSTOK I*, 1961, SOVIET UNION

**NUMBER OF HUMANS WHO HAVE TRAVELLED INTO SPACE SINCE THEN:** OVER 500

We've left Earth's surface, but we're still in the atmosphere – the thin gas blanket that covers the planet. It's divided into five layers that reach up to around 10,000 km (6,200 mi). We're currently in the stratosphere layer, but looking down below us to the troposphere we can see the weather – and some pretty cool views of the planet!

That big swirling cloud below is definitely a hurricane. Gulp!

## ATMOSPHERE STATS

**LOCATION:** EARTH'S ATMOSPHERE, LOOKING DOWN ON A HURRICANE IN THE CARIBBEAN SEA

**TROPOSPHERE HEIGHT:** 0–14.5 KM (0–9 MI)

**TROPOSPHERE TEMPERATURE:** AVERAGE OF 15°C (59°F) AT GROUND LEVEL TO -57°C (-70°C) AT THE TOP

**STRATOSPHERE HEIGHT:** 14.5–50 KM (9–31 MI)

**STRATOSPHERE TEMPERATURE:** -51°C (-60°F) AT THE BOTTOM TO -15°C (5°F) AT THE TOP

**TOP RECORDED HURRICANE WIND SPEED:** 310 KPH (192 MPH)

# NIGHT LIGHTS

We've now reached the mesosphere – the third layer of Earth's atmosphere. Up here, we've got to avoid small lumps of space rock travelling towards the planet at 72,000 kph (45,000 mph). Luckily, particles in the atmosphere rub against these meteoroids, heating them, and causing them to burn up, so hopefully we can just sit back and watch these 'shooting stars'!

We can also, see dancing green bands of light in the thermosphere above us – known as the Aurora Borealis in the northern hemisphere, and the Aurora Australis in the southern. They occur when high-energy particles from the Sun collide with atoms in the atmosphere.

Bang! That's another meteoroid hitting the space mobile. Where are they coming from?

They are usually stray bits of the Asteroid Belt, or occasionally bits of the Moon or Mars.

## ATMOSPHERE STATS

**LOCATION:** MESOSPHERE, EARTH'S ATMOSPHERE, LOOKING DOWN ON THE CITY LIGHTS OF SWEDEN AND DENMARK

**MESOSPHERE HEIGHT:** 50–85 KM (31–53 MI)

**MESOSPHERE TEMPERATURE:**
-15°C TO -140°C (5°F TO -220°F)

**THERMOSPHERE HEIGHT:** 85–600 KM (53–373 MI)

**THERMOSPHERE TEMPERATURE:**
500°C TO 2,000°C (932°F TO 3,632°F)

**AURORA COLOURS:** GREEN, PINK, YELLOW, BLUE, VIOLET

# SPACE WALK

There's no turning back now, we've officially left Earth and crossed into space. We're in a cold **vacuum**, with no air and, as we're in orbit, we can't feel gravity's pull – we're weightless! It's time to put on our Manned Maneuvering Units (MMUs) so we can safely space walk outside the space mobile and make any repairs. The MMU supplies us with air, water, protection and, most importantly, a jet-pack to allow us to move around!

The MMU has it all: a life support system with liquids, oxygen and temperature control, gas thrusters to move us around and joysticks so we can control our movements.

## SPACE WALK STATS

**LOCATION:** SPACE, OVER 100 KM (62 MI) ABOVE EARTH

**FIRST TETHERED SPACE WALK:** ALEXEY LEONOV, 1965, SOVIET UNION

**MMU POWER:** NITROGEN GAS THRUSTERS

**MMU WEIGHT:** 140 KG (310 LBS)

**MMU SPEED:** USUALLY CRAWLING PACE, BUT CAN ACCELERATE TO 72 KPH (45 MPH)

**LONGEST SPACE WALK:** 8 HOURS 56 MINUTES BY SUSAN HELMS AND JAMES VOSS, 2001, USA

**MOST SPACE WALKS:** 16 (AMOUNTING TO OVER 82 HOURS) BY ANATOLY SOLOVYEV, 1988-1998, SOVIET UNION

Usually space walks are tethered – the astronauts are connected to their spacecraft by a cable. The first untethered space walk in an MMU was by the American astronaut Bruce McCandless in 1984.

Wait for me! It took ages to get into this with all the undergarments and double-checking that the oxygen supply works!

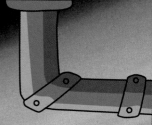

You can clearly see the thin layers of Earth's atmosphere from up here. Space is said to begin 100 km (62 mi) above the planet's surface.

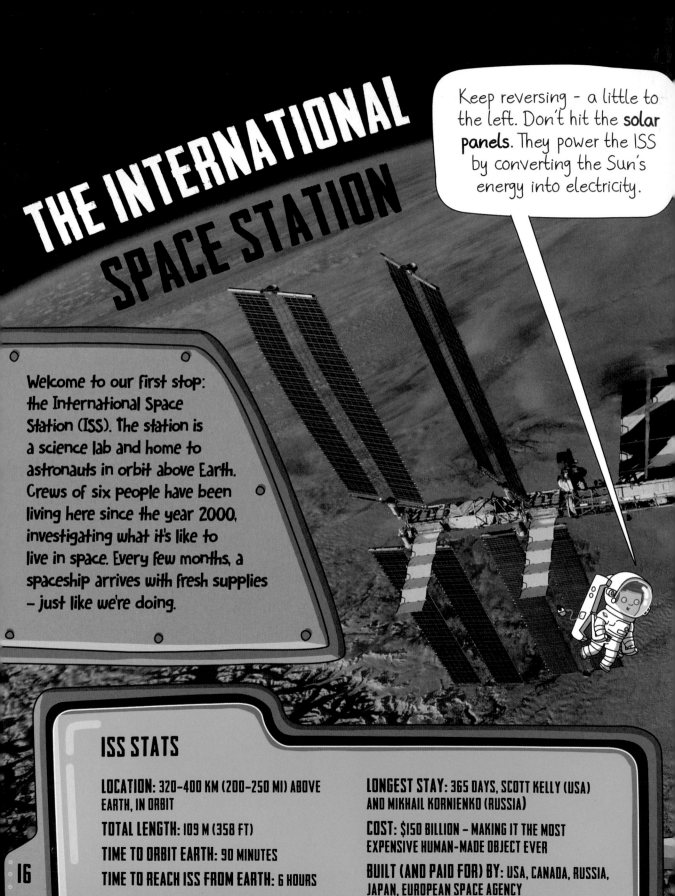

# THE INTERNATIONAL SPACE STATION

Keep reversing – a little to the left. Don't hit the **solar panels**. They power the ISS by converting the Sun's energy into electricity.

Welcome to our first stop: the International Space Station (ISS). The station is a science lab and home to astronauts in orbit above Earth. Crews of six people have been living here since the year 2000, investigating what it's like to live in space. Every few months, a spaceship arrives with fresh supplies – just like we're doing.

## ISS STATS

**LOCATION:** 320–400 KM (200–250 MI) ABOVE EARTH, IN ORBIT

**TOTAL LENGTH:** 109 M (358 FT)

**TIME TO ORBIT EARTH:** 90 MINUTES

**TIME TO REACH ISS FROM EARTH:** 6 HOURS

**LONGEST STAY:** 365 DAYS, SCOTT KELLY (USA) AND MIKHAIL KORNIENKO (RUSSIA)

**COST:** $150 BILLION – MAKING IT THE MOST EXPENSIVE HUMAN-MADE OBJECT EVER

**BUILT (AND PAID FOR) BY:** USA, CANADA, RUSSIA, JAPAN, EUROPEAN SPACE AGENCY

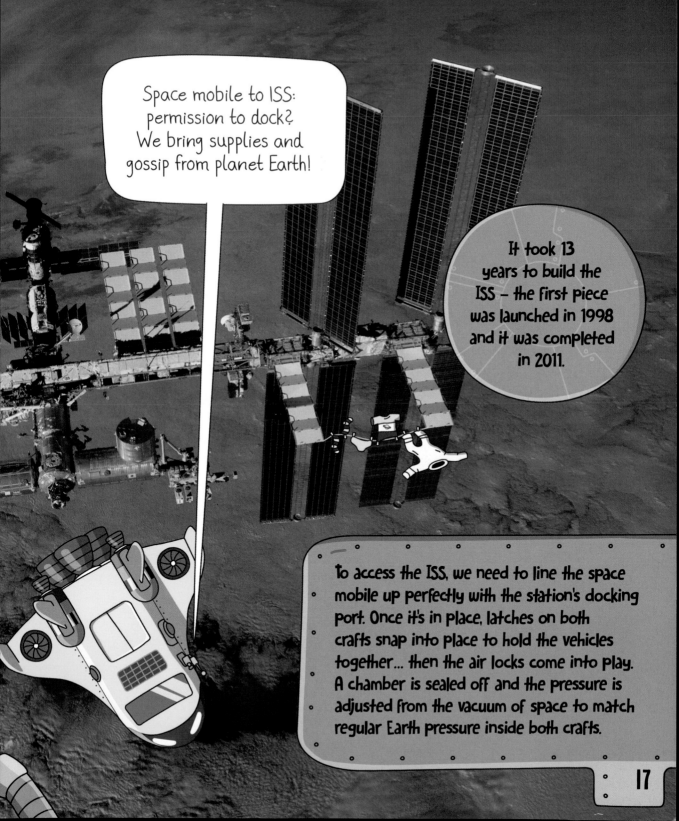

Space mobile to ISS: permission to dock? We bring supplies and gossip from planet Earth!

It took 13 years to build the ISS – the first piece was launched in 1998 and it was completed in 2011.

To access the ISS, we need to line the space mobile up perfectly with the station's docking port. Once it's in place, latches on both crafts snap into place to hold the vehicles together... then the air locks come into play. A chamber is sealed off and the pressure is adjusted from the vacuum of space to match regular Earth pressure inside both crafts.

# FLOATING IN THE

# SPACE STATION

Woah! We're floating, but not because of the lack of gravity. There's lots of gravity up here. In fact, the ISS is constantly falling towards the Earth, pulled by gravity. But it's also flying round the planet at 27,600 kph (17,150 mph), which matches the curve of the Earth, so it never hits it. It is this constant falling that makes everyone feel weightless. This is known as microgravity.

## SPACE STATS

LOCATION: INSIDE ISS

FIRST PERSON TO UNDERSTAND GRAVITY: SIR ISAAC NEWTON

GRAVITY DEFINITION: THE ATTRACTION BETWEEN ANY TWO MASSES

EFFECTS OF WEIGHTLESSNESS ON HUMANS: PUFFY HEAD AND SKINNY LEGS, MUSCLE AND BONE DENSITY LOSS, LESS COMPRESSED SPINE, CONFUSION, SPACE SICKNESS

In microgravity, your muscles don't hold you up, so you need to exercise every day to keep them strong.

In microgravity, everything seems weightless – so eating and drinking can be a little tricky when every crumb, drop of water, or squeeze of toothpaste can go floating off. Our space mobile has a special device that recreates Earth's gravity so we don't float around.

# THE HUBBLE SPACE TELESCOPE

Meet the most far-sighted object in space – it's even looked back in time! The Hubble Space Telescope has none of Earth's weather or hazy atmosphere to block its view of the universe, and has taken over 1.3 million observations since its launch in 1990. To get its images, Hubble must stay extremely steady – once it locks onto a target it only wobbles the equivalent of the width of a hair viewed from 1.6 km (1 mi) away!

It was named after the American astronomer, Edwin Hubble. Let me take a selfie!

A new, even more powerful device, the James Webb Space Telescope, is due to be launched in 2021.

## HUBBLE TELESCOPE STATS

**LOCATION:** 550 KM (340 MI) ABOVE EARTH, IN ORBIT

**LAUNCH:** 24TH APRIL 1990

**LENGTH:** 13.3 M (43.5 FT)

**SPEED:** 27,000 KPH (17,000 MPH)

**TIME TO ORBIT EARTH:** 95 MINUTES

**DISTANCE TRAVELLED AROUND EARTH:** OVER 4.8 BILLION KM (3 BILLION MI)

**PRIMARY MIRROR DIAMETER:** 2.4 M (94.5 IN)

**NUMBER OF OBJECTS OBSERVED:** OVER 38,000

Perhaps Hubble's most amazing pictures are the Deep Field images, first taken in 1995. They show the furthest galaxies ever seen — some are 13 billion **light years** away, which means we are looking at them as they were, 13 billion years ago! The images cover just a small section of the sky, but there are almost 3,000 galaxies in this picture alone!

# SPACE JUNK

## SPACE STATS

**LOCATION:** 36,000 KM (22,400 MI) ABOVE EARTH, IN ORBIT

**FIRST SATELLITE IN SPACE:** *SPUTNIK I*, LAUNCHED IN 1957 BY THE SOVIET UNION

**MOST COMMON USE FOR SATELLITES:** COMMUNICATIONS

**OLDEST PIECE OF ORBITING SPACE JUNK:** *VANGUARD I*, LAUNCHED IN 1958 BY THE USA

**TRACKED PIECES OF DEBRIS:** 500,000 PIECES

**RATE OF DEBRIS RETURNING TO EARTH:** ONLY ONE PIECE A DAY

Yikes, there's so much disused stuff orbiting Earth that it's like flying through a floating rubbish dump. Like everything else in orbit, the objects are moving at around 28,000 kph (17,500 mph), so even the smallest chunk can cause major damage if it collides with us. There are 20,000 pieces larger than a softball, 500,000 the size of a marble, and millions of small pieces.

Even tiny paint flecks chipped off satellites have caused major damage to spacecraft windows in the past.

A low-orbiting satellite can be sent back to Earth to burn up in the atmosphere. But if it's in high orbit, it may be sent into 'graveyard orbit', 320 km (200 mi) beyond the highest active satellites. That is what's created this cosmic rubbish dump. As the satellites disintegrate, they create smaller pieces of space junk.

Let's do our bit to tidy up by operating the space mobile's rubbish net.

# LANDING ON THE MOON

Welcome to the Moon! Only 12 people have ever landed here, the first being Neil Armstrong in 1969. The six manned Apollo missions that reached the Moon's surface between 1969 and 1972 did so in small lunar modules, while a main craft stayed in orbit. Afterwards, the top half of each lunar module blasted off to rejoin the main craft, leaving the bottom half back on the Moon, where it remains to this day.

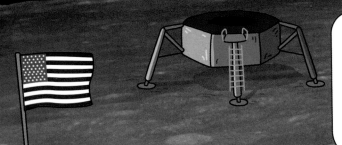

NEIL RULES

Look! We can see the Earth beyond the Moon's horizon. People call this an 'Earthrise'.

The Moon doesn't have a protective atmosphere, so rocks from space often hit its surface, churning up a fine lunar dust. This dust may look powdery, but it can be as sharp as glass. If you breathe it in, it could shred your insides! Don't take your helmet off!

# EXPLORING THE MOON

As Earth's closest neighbour, the Moon has been visited several times by spacecraft – but only six of these missions have put people on the surface. The final three Apollo missions carried out by NASA also carried a lunar rover with them. The space mobile has its own brand new rover vehicle, so this is the perfect place to get it up and running.

Oh look, I've put a new battery in this old lunar rover and it still works!

The Moon's surface is covered in craters made by asteroid impacts billions of years ago. Unlike Earth, the Moon has no atmosphere so the craters haven't weathered away.

The rovers were designed to take the Apollo astronauts away from their lunar module in order to sample rocks from different places on the Moon's surface. But the astronauts made sure not to drive too far, so they could always get back to their module in case of rover failure. No one wants a stranded astronaut!

I've heard that future moon buggies will be more advanced, so astronauts can live and work in them.

The lunar rovers used on the Moon were built like dirt buggies, with wire-mesh tyres for extra grip. The craters on the surface make for a bouncy ride!

## LUNAR ROVER STATS

**LOCATION:** MOON

**LUNAR ROVER LENGTH:** 3.1 M (10.2 FT)

**HEIGHT:** 1.1 M (3.6 FT)

**MASS:** 210 KG (463 LBS)

**TOP RECORDED SPEED:** 18 KPH (11.2 MPH)

**MAX DRIVE TIME:** 4 HOURS 26 MINUTES (ON THE APOLLO 17 MISSION IN 1972)

# THE SUN

The Sun's core is 15 million°C (27 million°F). That's off the scale!

We're headed to the centre of the Solar System and boy is it HOT! Our local star, the Sun, is a giant ball of burning gas. Its enormous gravity keeps everything in the Solar System orbiting around it. The Sun creates its own energy through a powerful process called nuclear fusion. It is the transfer of this energy, in the form of heat and light, that allows life to exist on Earth.

According to scientists, the Sun is a yellow dwarf star – but, close up, it seems like a giant rather than a dwarf!

Out in front, we can see giant loops of glowing gas called plasma erupting from the Sun's surface. These can extend for 200,000 km (125,000 mi), spraying material out into space. Looking at an **ultraviolet** image on this smaller screen, I can also see swirling storms, called solar storms, on the Sun's surface.

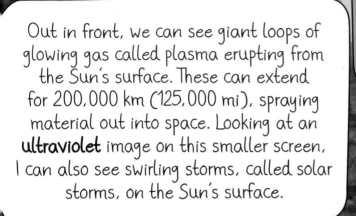

## SUN STATS

**LOCATION:** THE SUN

**SURFACE TEMPERATURE:** 5,500°C (9,900°F)

**DIAMETER:** 1.39 MILLION KM (864,000 MI) OR 109 TIMES THE SIZE OF EARTH

**AGE:** 4.5 BILLION YEARS. IT WILL EXIST FOR ANOTHER 5 BILLION YEARS

**TIME TO ROTATE (AT THE EQUATOR):** ABOUT 27 EARTH DAYS

**TIME FOR THE SUN'S LIGHT TO REACH EARTH:** 8 MINUTES

The image on Junko's screen shows just how big the Sun is compared to the planets. It contains 99.8% of all the Solar System's mass.

# MERCURY

Both the smallest planet and the one closest to the Sun, Mercury's surface can reach a scorching 430°C (800°F) in the sunshine. But what the travel guide didn't tell us is that it's also a freezing –180°C (–290°F) in the shade! This is all because there is no atmosphere on Mercury to absorb the heat from the Sun. It has a solid, cratered surface, a bit like the Moon.

Brrr! It's freezing over here in the shadows. I need some extra layers.

Mercury is named after the fastest of the Roman gods due to its speedy orbit around the Sun.

The *Mariner 10* and *Messenger* spacecraft are the only vehicles from Earth to have flown past Mercury so far, which means our space mobile is the first mission to land!

Good job I remembered my sunglasses. The sunlight here is 11 times brighter than on Earth!

## MERCURY STATS

**LOCATION:** MERCURY

**DIAMETER:** 4,879 KM (3,032 MI)

**LENGTH OF YEAR:** 88 EARTH DAYS

**LENGTH OF DAY:** 59 EARTH DAYS

**SPEED OF ORBIT:** 47 KM (29 MI) PER SECOND

**TIME FOR SUNLIGHT TO REACH MERCURY:** 3 MINUTES, 13 SECONDS

# VENUS

We need to be quick so we don't end up like *Venera 13*, the last probe to visit in 1982 – it was destroyed by Venus' atmosphere in just two hours. In fact, we'd better stay inside the space mobile... the surface is covered in volcanoes, the air is thick with sulphuric acid clouds, and the atmosphere is 97% **carbon dioxide**, which traps the heat making it an unbearable 460°C (860°F) on the surface.

## VENUS STATS

**LOCATION:** VENUS

**DIAMETER:** 12,104 KM (7,521 MI)

**LENGTH OF YEAR:** 225 EARTH DAYS

**LENGTH OF DAY:** 243 EARTH DAYS

**DISTANCE FROM THE SUN:** 108 MILLION KM (67 MILLION MI)

**TIME FOR SUNLIGHT TO REACH VENUS:** 6 MINUTES

**TALLEST VOLCANO:** MAAT MONS, 8 KM (5 MI)

... a stormy place
– lightning bolts light up
the clouds, which are filled
with acidic raindrops.

Venus is curious in that
it spins in the opposite
direction to Earth, so
the Sun rises in the
west! It also spins very
slowly, taking 243 days
to complete one rotation.
Meanwhile, it takes just
225 days to orbit the
Sun, meaning that Venus'
day is actually longer
than its year.

Don't open the door! The
atmosphere is thick enough to
crush you, and the heat can melt
lead – as well as us!

Even the space mobile's umbrella is
struggling to cope with the acid in
the atmosphere. Time to leave!

# MARS

Next stop is the red planet, Mars. It gets its colour from the rusty iron minerals in the surface soil. When this dusty soil gets kicked up into the atmosphere by storms, it can make the whole planet look fuzzy. Mars is a cold, desert-like planet, but it does have seasons and weather, as well as volcanoes, canyons and ice caps, so it's well worth a visit.

That spacecraft up ahead is the *Mars Reconnaissance Orbiter*, which has been flying round the planet since 2006, taking pictures and gathering information.

More than half of the missions to Mars have been unsuccessful – so we need to be careful!

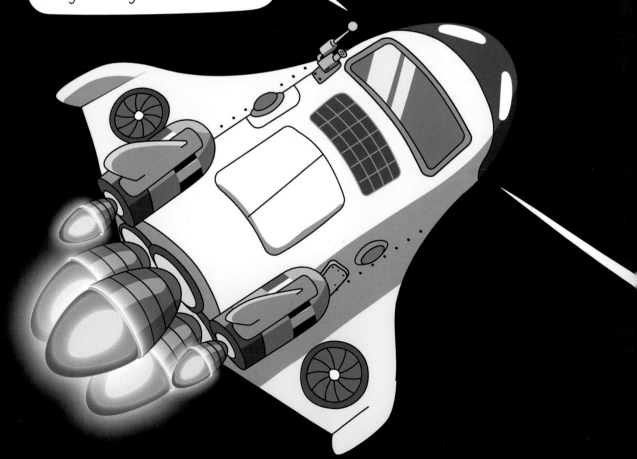

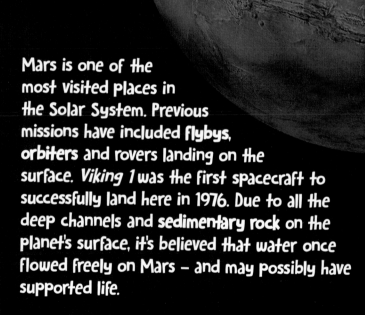

Mars is one of the most visited places in the Solar System. Previous missions have included flybys, orbiters and rovers landing on the surface. *Viking 1* was the first spacecraft to successfully land here in 1976. Due to all the deep channels and **sedimentary rock** on the planet's surface, it's believed that water once flowed freely on Mars – and may possibly have supported life.

Mars is named after the Greek god of war because it looks like the colour of blood!

## MARS STATS

**LOCATION:** MARS

**DIAMETER:** 6,779 KM (4,212 MI)

**LENGTH OF YEAR:** 687 EARTH DAYS

**LENGTH OF DAY:** 24.6 EARTH HOURS

**DISTANCE FROM THE SUN:** 228 MILLION KM (142 MILLION MI)

**TIME FOR SUNLIGHT TO REACH MARS:** 12.6 MINUTES

**MOONS:** 2 - PHOBOS AND DEIMOS

# OLYMPUS MONS

Keep climbing, Junko, I want to reach the top of Mars before sunset! Olympus Mons is the largest peak in the Solar System at 25,000 m (82,020 ft) high. It's long been thought to be an extinct volcano, but scientists now think that Olympus Mons and three smaller nearby volcanoes may just be dormant, waiting for the moment when hot **magma** surges up through them again.

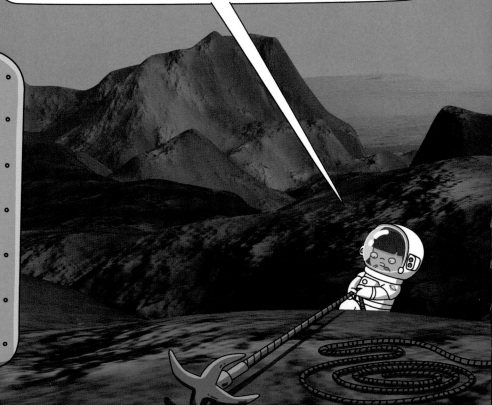

I thought climbing Mount Everest on planet Earth was a challenge, but Olympus Mons is three times as tall! Good job I only weigh one-third of my Earth weight to make this climb easier!

Olympus Mons is part of a group of volcanoes near to Mars' **equator**. They are so high, they tower above the dust storms on the surface of the planet. So this is the place to be if you want to escape a storm.

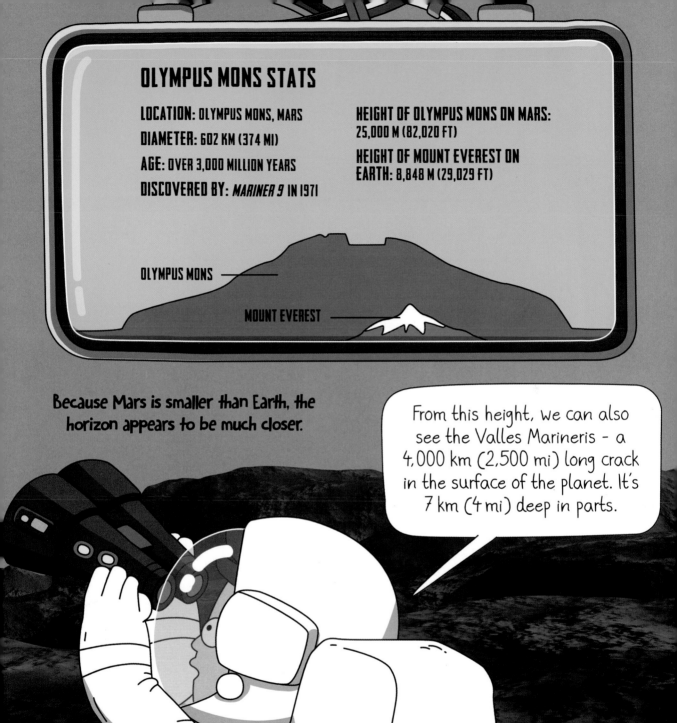

## OLYMPUS MONS STATS

**LOCATION:** OLYMPUS MONS, MARS

**DIAMETER:** 602 KM (374 MI)

**AGE:** OVER 3,000 MILLION YEARS

**DISCOVERED BY:** *MARINER 9* IN 1971

**HEIGHT OF OLYMPUS MONS ON MARS:** 25,000 M (82,020 FT)

**HEIGHT OF MOUNT EVEREST ON EARTH:** 8,848 M (29,029 FT)

OLYMPUS MONS —————

MOUNT EVEREST —————

Because Mars is smaller than Earth, the horizon appears to be much closer.

From this height, we can also see the Valles Marineris – a 4,000 km (2,500 mi) long crack in the surface of the planet. It's 7 km (4 mi) deep in parts.

# MEET A ROVER

We're the first humans on Mars, but we're not the first visitors. Four Martian rovers have explored the planet before us, and there are plans to send another in a few years time.

Say 'cheese', Curiosity!

Opportunity was designed to operate for 90 days, but has been going for over 14 years. It has travelled over 45 km (28 mi).

The microwave-sized *Sojourner* was the first rover to arrive in 1997. It was followed in 2004 by *Spirit* and *Opportunity*. The size of golf buggies, they landed on different sides of the planet, but both found evidence of water! The most recent rover, *Curiosity*, landed in 2012. The size of a car, its mission is to examine the planet's rocks to discover if there were once the ingredients to allow life on Mars.

*Curiosity* is almost as hi-tech as the space mobile's rover! It has cameras, a **spectrometer**, a range of sensors and it's powered by nuclear batteries.

## ROVER STATS

**LOCATION:** AEOLIS MONS, MARS

**WEIGHT:** 900 KG (1,984 LBS)

**LENGTH:** 3 M (9.8 FT) LONG, 2.8 M (9.1 FT) TALL

**TOP SPEED:** 5 CM PER SECOND (2 IN PER SECOND)

**AVERAGE DISTANCE TRAVELLED EACH DAY:** 200 M (660 FT)

**NUMBER OF CAMERAS:** 17

# THE ASTEROID BELT

The next stop on our planetary tour is Jupiter, but the flight path is not exactly clear! Between planets four and five in our Solar System are thousands of lumps of rock, orbiting the Sun in an area called the Asteroid Belt. These lumps of rock are remains from the formation of the Solar System, but they are too small to be classed as planets. The very largest, Ceres, which we're passing now, is known as a dwarf planet.

Launched in 2007, the spacecraft *Dawn* has studied two Asteroid Belt bodies: Vesta and Ceres. And it might be my body next if I don't get out of the way soon!

Ceres is a large crater-covered ball of rock and ice. On its surface are several mysterious bright spots. No one is quite sure what makes these spots look so shiny – they could be pockets containing ice or salt, perhaps produced by icy volcanoes erupting on the surface.

Ceres has been called a comet, a planet, an asteroid and a dwarf planet since it was first spotted in 1801. But it was officially classed as a dwarf planet in 2006.

## ASTEROID BELT STATS

**LOCATION:** ASTEROID BELT

**ASTEROIDS LARGER THAN 1 KM (0.6 MI) IN BELT:** 1.9 MILLION

**ASTEROIDS WITH A MOON:** OVER 150 THAT WE KNOW OF

**CERES RADIUS:** 946 KM (588 MI)

**LENGTH OF YEAR:** 4.6 EARTH YEARS

**LENGTH OF DAY:** 9 EARTH HOURS

**LENGTH OF DAWN SPACECRAFT:** 2.36 M (7.7 FT)

Some scientists think these bright spots may be 'cryovolcanoes' - volcanoes that erupt water or gas. Let's turn the searchlights on and have a closer look.

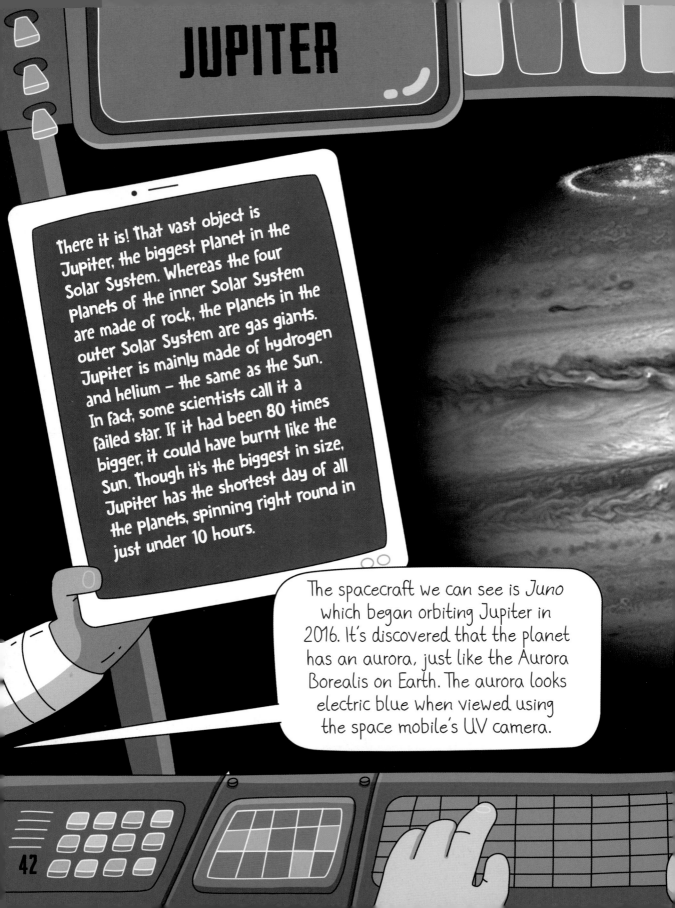

There it is! That vast object is Jupiter, the biggest planet in the Solar System. Whereas the four planets of the inner Solar System are made of rock, the planets in the outer Solar System are gas giants. Jupiter is mainly made of hydrogen and helium – the same as the Sun. In fact, some scientists call it a failed star. If it had been 80 times bigger, it could have burnt like the Sun. Though it's the biggest in size, Jupiter has the shortest day of all the planets, spinning right round in just under 10 hours.

The spacecraft we can see is *Juno* which began orbiting Jupiter in 2016. It's discovered that the planet has an aurora, just like the Aurora Borealis on Earth. The aurora looks electric blue when viewed using the space mobile's UV camera.

## JUPITER STATS

**LOCATION:** JUPITER
**RADIUS:** 139,822 KM (86,881 MI)
**LENGTH OF YEAR:** 12 EARTH YEARS
**LENGTH OF DAY:** 10 EARTH HOURS
**MOONS:** 53 WITH NAMES, AT LEAST 79 IN TOTAL
**TIME FOR SUNLIGHT TO REACH JUPITER:** 43 MINUTES

When you line up the eight planets side-by-side, it's clear that Jupiter dwarfs the others. In fact, all seven other planets could fit inside it. No wonder it is named after the Roman king of the gods. Jupiter's clouds of gas swirl around it in a range of colours.

# THE GREAT RED SPOT

Junko, did you see the big red spot just below the equator of Jupiter? Well, we're now right above it, and the swirling clouds are beginning to spin us around. The spot is a huge storm that was first spotted over 185 years ago - but it has probably been raging for much longer. We'd better put the space mobile into warp speed to fly past it!

## GREAT RED SPOT STATS

LOCATION: GREAT RED SPOT, JUPITER

WIDTH: APPROX. 15,000 KM (9,320 MI)

ROTATION SPEED: 6 EARTH DAYS

COLOURS: SALMON, RED, ORANGE, GREY

NUMBER OF EARTHS THAT COULD FIT INSIDE THE GREAT RED SPOT: 2, PREVIOUSLY 3

The spot constantly moves around the planet sandwiched between two jet streams of gases, although it always stays the same distance from the equator. It's around double the size of Earth, but has actually shrunk over the past few decades, and may eventually disappear completely.

Woah, we're being spun by powerful winds. With speeds of between 435 and 685 kph (270–425 mph), this storm is more ferocious than any hurricane on Earth. It's also really cold – around -162°C (-260°F), while the rest of the planet is 'only' -148°C (-234°F).

# JUPITER'S MOONS

Jupiter's size means it has a strong gravitational pull. So, it's no surprise that it holds at least 79 moons in orbit around it. Some of these moons are giants and others are the size of small asteroids. The biggest four moons are shown on the screens here. They were first spotted by astronomer Galileo Galilei in 1610 and are called the Galilean satellites.

GANYMEDE

IO

EUROPA

CALLISTO

## GANYMEDE FACTS

DIAMETER: 5,268 KM (3,273 MI)
LARGE ENOUGH TO BE A PLANET
IF IT WEREN'T IN JUPITER'S ORBIT,
IT HAS ITS OWN MAGNETIC FIELD.

## CALLISTO FACTS

DIAMETER: 4,821 KM (2,996 MI)
ALL ITS CRATERS ARE DUE
TO ASTEROID IMPACTS MADE
THROUGHOUT HISTORY.

Ganymede is the biggest moon in the Solar System (it's even bigger than the planet Mercury). Callisto is covered in craters, while Io has lots of active volcanoes. Europa, the moon we're flying over now, is an icy body, but it may have water below its surface. It certainly looks like water shooting out of that **geyser**!

Scientists want to see if it's possible for life to exist in Europa's waters!

## IO FACTS

**DIAMETER:** 3,643 KM (2,264 MI)
THIS IS THE MOST VOLCANICALLY ACTIVE BODY IN THE ENTIRE SOLAR SYSTEM.

## EUROPA FACTS

**DIAMETER:** 3,122 KM (1,940 MI)
SCIENTISTS BELIEVE THERE MIGHT BE TWICE AS MUCH WATER HERE AS ON EARTH!

# SATURN

Saturn is so light and airy, it would float in a bucket of water – if you could find one big enough to hold it!

We're trying to collect samples of the lumps of rock and ice that orbit Saturn, forming its rings. Some are tiny, while others can be 10 m (30 ft) across. We need to make sure these moving chunks don't damage the space mobile! The planet itself is made up of gas and liquid surrounding a small solid core. But the enormous pressure means there's no chance of us actually landing on Saturn!

Let's fly to the Cassini Division. It's a gap 4,700 km (2,920 mi) wide between two of the rings and will reduce the risk of us being hit by one of these rocks!

When viewed from a long way away, Saturn's rings sparkle in the Sun's light and give the planet its distinctive look. But up close they are just chunks of ice and rock, held in orbit around the planet. There are seven main rings in total, each made of many smaller ones. The rings are probably made of broken pieces of comets, asteroids or moons.

I read that the ring system extends up to 282,000 km (175,000 mi) from the planet, but look — their vertical height is only about 10 m (30 ft)!

## SATURN STATS

**LOCATION:** SATURN

**DIAMETER:** 116,464 KM (72,367 MI)

**LENGTH OF YEAR:** 29.4 EARTH YEARS

**LENGTH OF DAY:** 10.7 EARTH HOURS

**TIME FOR SUNLIGHT TO REACH SATURN:** 83 MINUTES

**MOONS:** 53 CONFIRMED, 9 PROVISIONAL

**VISITORS:** *CASSINI* ORBITED SATURN 294 TIMES BETWEEN 2004 AND 2017

# TITAN

Welcome to Titan, Saturn's largest moon and the second largest moon in the Solar System. Titan is the only place other than Earth to have rivers, lakes and seas on its surface! However, they're not made of water, like on Earth. They're formed of liquid methane and ethane. Swimming in this liquid is not an enjoyable experience – it's freezing!

It looks like it's going to rain. When it does, some of the drops of liquid will then evaporate (turn into a gas), forming hazy clouds above us, just like water does on Earth.

The data that the *Huygens* probe collected tells us that Titan's core is rock, surrounded by a shell of water ice. Then there's a layer of salty liquid water and an outer crust of water ice. Scientists think there might also be liquid water volcanoes and perhaps even an underground ocean just 55–80 km (35–50 mi) below the surface.

## TITAN STATS

**LOCATION:** TITAN, SATURN'S MOON
**DIAMETER:** 5,150 KM (3,200 MI)
**DISTANCE FROM SATURN:** 1.2 MILLION KM (759,000 MI)
**TIME FOR SUNLIGHT TO REACH TITAN:** 80 MINUTES
**TIME TO ORBIT SATURN:** 15 DAYS, 22 HOURS
**SURFACE TEMPERATURE:** -179.5°C (-290°F)
**HUYGENS PROBE DIAMETER:** 2.7 M (9 FT)
**HUYGENS PROBE MASS:** 318 KG (700 LBS)

Hello, *Huygens!* This probe landed on Titan on the 14th January 2005. It survived for 72 minutes on the surface, and so it holds the record for the furthest landing from Earth – although I think we may beat that!

# URANUS

We're on Miranda, one of Uranus' moons, and the view is spectacular! Over there is Uranus, the planet known for its sideways rotation. It's believed a collision with an Earth-sized object knocked the planet on its side millions of years ago. Uranus' lovely bluey colour is caused by the methane in the atmosphere.

Wow, that's Verona Rupes, the tallest cliff in the Solar System. At nearly 20 km (12 mi) high, it's taller than Mount Everest, and this canyon below it is five times the depth of the Grand Canyon on Earth.

Miranda is one of Uranus' 27 moons, and many are named after characters from Shakespeare's plays. Some of Uranus' moons are called 'shepherd moons' as they orbit near to the planet's rings, keeping the dust and ice that form them in position.

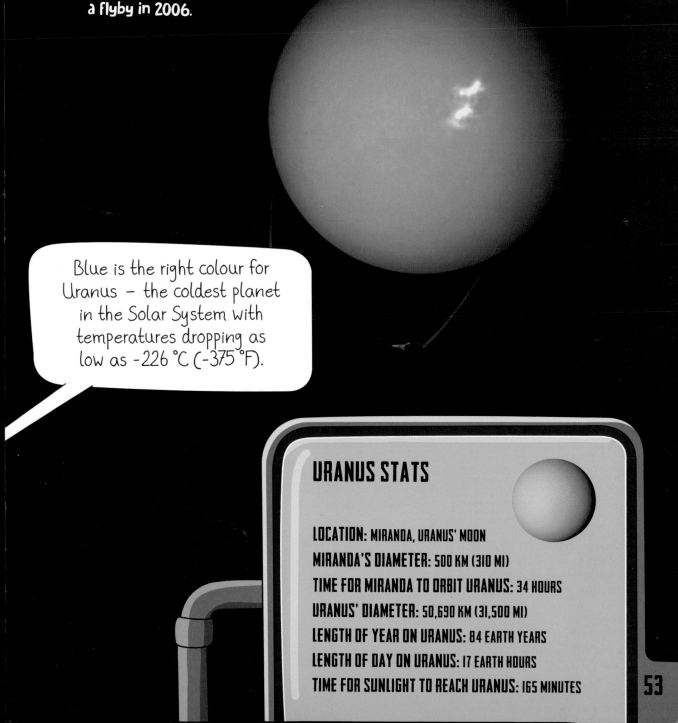

Blue is the right colour for Uranus – the coldest planet in the Solar System with temperatures dropping as low as -226 °C (-375 °F).

## URANUS STATS

**LOCATION:** MIRANDA, URANUS' MOON
**MIRANDA'S DIAMETER:** 500 KM (310 MI)
**TIME FOR MIRANDA TO ORBIT URANUS:** 34 HOURS
**URANUS' DIAMETER:** 50,690 KM (31,500 MI)
**LENGTH OF YEAR ON URANUS:** 84 EARTH YEARS
**LENGTH OF DAY ON URANUS:** 17 EARTH HOURS
**TIME FOR SUNLIGHT TO REACH URANUS:** 165 MINUTES

# NEPTUNE

Hold onto your hats, we're approaching the windiest part of the Solar System – the planet Neptune. This is the furthest planet from the Sun and a cold, dark world. Clouds of frozen methane gas, which make the planet look blue, are spun around the globe at 2,000 kph (1,200 mph). In fact, astronomers spotted one cloud, called 'Scooter', that whizzed around the globe in just 16 hours. The Hubble Telescope discovered a huge vortex of clouds as well.

Triton, the big moon we're flying past now, is the only large moon to circle in the opposite direction to its planet's rotation. When it flew past, Voyager 2 also spotted two geysers shooting up icy material 8 km (5 mi) into the atmosphere above Triton. Due to the distance from the Sun, it's freezing here.

Neptune is named after the god of the sea in Greek mythology, and Triton was his son.

Neptune has seasons like Earth, but each one lasts for 40 years.

Neptune previously had a Great Dark Spot on its surface. It was a storm that raged for five years and was large enough to gobble up Earth.

## NEPTUNE STATS

LOCATION: NEPTUNE

DIAMETER: 49,244 KM (30,598 MI)

LENGTH OF YEAR: 165 EARTH YEARS

LENGTH OF DAY: 16 EARTH HOURS

MOONS: 13 CONFIRMED

RINGS: 5

TIME FOR SUNLIGHT TO REACH NEPTUNE: 4 HOURS

# PLUTO

Poor Pluto – from here, the Sun looks very far away. It was also downgraded from a planet to a dwarf planet in 2006. We've stopped off on Charon, its biggest moon, to take a look at some of Pluto's features, including a beautiful heart-shaped region of frozen nitrogen. Can you spot it?

Pluto has an interesting path round the Sun. It follows an orbit that is much more oval-shaped than the planets. This means it constantly changes its distance from the Sun. At its furthest point it is 7.3 billion km (4.5 billion mi) away, but at its closest point, it is nearer than Neptune.

# COMETS

Hold steady, Eddie! I want to take a picture of this comet. These frozen lumps of rock, dust and gas are leftovers from the formation of the Solar System. When a comet nears the Sun, it heats up and develops a cloud called a coma around it. This coma is blown out behind it to form a double tail — one made of dust and the other of gas.

## COMET STATS

**LOCATION:** OUTER SOLAR SYSTEM

**SIZE OF HALLEY'S COMET:** 15 KM (9 MI) LONG

**SPEED OF HALLEY'S COMET WHEN IN THE KUIPER BELT:** 1 KM (0.6 MI) PER SECOND

**SPEED OF HALLEY'S COMET WHEN NEAR THE SUN:** 50 KM (30 MI) PER SECOND

**DIRECTION OF COMET TAILS:** THEY ALWAYS FACE AWAY FROM THE SUN

Most comets originate in an area surrounding the Solar System, known as the Oort cloud. Each comet follows a different path. Short-period comets take less than 200 years to orbit the Sun. However, the orbits of some long-period comets can take up to 30 million years.

Junko, I remember seeing a comet in the night sky on Earth! One of the most famous is Halley's Comet, which passes by our planet every 76 years.

Comets have a frozen nucleus that is a few kilometres wide, but their tails can become thousands of kilometres long.

# VOYAGER 1

Look, a fellow spacecraft! This is *Voyager 1*, the furthest human-made object from Earth. We've now left the Solar System and entered interstellar space – the area between planetary systems in a galaxy. *Voyager 1's* mission was initially just to observe the outer planets, but it keeps on flying and it's now 'only' 40,000 years until it comes close to another star!

Maybe we're the first to dance in space! Let's enjoy this moment, as who knows what dangers we'll discover beyond our Solar System.

We've found the famous golden record! It was placed on board *Voyager 1* as a greeting to any form of life that found it. It's filled with photos and sounds from Earth, as well as music.

*Voyager 1* and its sister, *Voyager 2*, are whizzing along at 61,000 kph (38,000 mph). They have told us much about the outer Solar System so far, but we rely on telescopes for information beyond this point.

## VOYAGER 1 STATS

**LOCATION:** INTERSTELLAR SPACE

**LAUNCH DATE:** 5TH SEPTEMBER 1977

**DATE IT ENTERED INTERSTELLAR SPACE:** AUGUST 2012

**DISTANCE FROM THE SUN:** OVER 21 BILLION KM (13 BILLION MI)

**GOLDEN RECORD CONTAINS:** 115 IMAGES, 55 LANGUAGES AND 90 MINUTES OF MUSIC

# EXOPLANETS

We may be far from our Solar System's eight planets now, but that doesn't mean there aren't more out there to explore. Most stars have planets orbiting around them. We call them exoplanets and today we are visiting Proxima b, the closest known exoplanet to us. It's a little bigger than Earth, has a rocky surface and orbits the star Proxima Centauri.

Proxima b orbits in the 'habitable zone' around its star. This means the conditions are suitable for liquid water to exist on the surface of the planet. And if there's water, that also means life could exist!

The space mobile has highlighted some more planets in the Trappist-1 planetary system, around 39 light years from the Sun. All seven planets are roughly Earth-sized. Numbers four to six may have water on their surface as they are in the habitable zone!

## EXOPLANET STATS

**LOCATION:** PROXIMA B

**DISTANCE FROM EARTH:** 4.2 LIGHT YEARS

**DIAMETER:** APPROX. 7,000 KM (4,350 MI)

**STAR:** PROXIMA CENTAURI

**TIME TO ORBIT THE STAR:** 11.1 DAYS

**FIRST DISCOVERED:** AUGUST 2016

# GIANT STARS

Time to put our sunglasses on, we're passing Sirius A – the brightest star you can see from Earth. It's 20 times brighter than the Sun and about twice the size. But this is nothing compared to the size of some stars! Located 640 light years from Earth, Betelgeuse is one of the biggest stars we know of. If it took the place of our Sun, it would extend out to almost reach Jupiter.

What will happen to our Sun? Will it explode at the end of its life?

No. Right now, our Sun is a medium-sized star known as a yellow dwarf. In five billion years time, it will grow into a red giant. Then, when it runs out of fuel, it will shrink into a white dwarf. The blue star on the left is Sirius B, a white dwarf star.

## RELATIVE STAR SIZES

 Our Sun

• Sirius A

 Rigel

Betelgeuse

## STAR STATS

**LOCATION:** SIRIUS A
**DISTANCE FROM EARTH:** 8.1 LIGHT YEARS
**OTHER NAMES:** DOG STAR, ALPHA CANIS MAJOR
**DIAMETER:** 2.4 MILLION KM (1.5 MILLION MI)
**TEMPERATURE:** 10,000°C (18,000°F)
**SIRIUS B DIAMETER:** 11,800 KM (7,300 MI)
**SIRIUS B TEMPERATURE:** 25,000°C (45,000°F)

All stars grow in size when they reach the end of their life. While our Sun will expand into a red giant, stars that are over eight times the mass of the Sun grow into supergiants. Betelgeuse has already expanded to become a supergiant 950 times larger than the Sun. When it finally runs out of fuel, it will blow apart in a supernova.

We can just see our Sun off in in the distance.

# NEW STARS

Shh, don't wake the baby stars! Ahead is the Orion Nebula, a region where new stars are formed. We're now 1,500 light years from Earth. There are more than 3,000 stars within these vast clouds of dust and gas. The bright area in the centre is home to a group of stars known as the Trapezium.

This nebula is named Orion as it can be seen within the Orion **constellation** of stars in the sky above Earth.

A nebula is a giant cloud of dust and gas, mostly hydrogen and helium. Sometimes gravity can slowly draw this material together. As the clouds get denser, their gravity gets stronger. Eventually, the material collapses, creating heat. When the temperature reaches 4 million°C (18 million°F), a new star is born.

## ORION NEBULA STATS

**LOCATION:** ORION NEBULA (ALSO CALLED MESSIER 42)

**DISTANCE FROM EARTH:** 1,500 LIGHT YEARS

**DIAMETER:** 25 LIGHT YEARS

**AGE:** 2 MILLION YEARS OLD

**DISCOVERY DATE:** 1610

**STARS CURRENTLY BEING BORN IN THE NEBULA:** AROUND 1,000

The white arrow above shows the location of the nebula, just below Orion's belt.

I've used the tablet to zoom in on another nebula in this Orion constellation region. It's called the Horsehead Nebula because the dark clouds of dust look like a horse's head. The pink glow behind it is caused by hydrogen gas.

# EXPLOSION!

How pretty! This may look like a flower, but it's not very delicate. We're looking at the remains of a supernova – the explosion of a star. As a massive star begins to run out of fuel, it weakens until it can no longer support its own weight. Finally, it collapses causing the biggest type of explosion in the universe: a supernova. KABOOM!

Average-sized stars gradually throw off their layers of gas, forming red giant stars. Eventually, they become strange glowing shapes called planetary nebulas. This one, called the Helix Nebula, looks like a giant eye.

When a supernova explodes, it sends lots of cosmic debris into space, including **gamma rays** and intense heat, which could be dangerous for us. It's much safer now, but there are still lots of **X-rays** being shot out by the old core of the star, which is called a neutron star. Good job the space mobile has a thick shell.

## SUPERNOVA STATS

**LOCATION:** CASSIOPEIA A, SUPERNOVA REMNANT

**DISTANCE FROM EARTH:** 11,000 LIGHT YEARS

**DIAMETER:** 10 LIGHT YEARS

**SPEED OF EXPLOSION:** UP TO 40,000 KM A SECOND (25,000 MI PER SECOND)

**DATE THE EXPLOSION WAS VISIBLE FROM EARTH:** 1680

**ORIGINAL MASS OF THE STAR:** 16 TIMES THE SIZE OF THE SUN

This supernova remnant is called Cassiopeia A. The clouds of debris that are blasted from the explosion drift off into space and may go on to form nebulas and new stars.

A black hole forms when a dead star's core crushes in on itself. A massive star will collapse down to just a few kilometres across. Though small, it's incredibly dense with such a powerful gravitational pull that anything that gets close, even light, is pulled in and eventually disappears.

There's a supermassive black hole at the centre of the Milky Way galaxy, in a region called Sagittarius A.

## BLACK HOLE STATS

**LOCATION:** A BLACK HOLE AT THE CENTRE OF THE MILKY WAY

**NUMBER OF BLACK HOLES IN THE MILKY WAY:** TENS OF MILLIONS

**NEAREST BLACK HOLE TO EARTH:** 3,000 LIGHT YEARS AWAY

**FIRST BLACK HOLE DISCOVERED:** CYGNUS X-I, IN 1964

**TYPES OF BLACK HOLE:** PRIMORDIAL (SMALL), STELLAR (MEDIUM), SUPERMASSIVE (LARGE)

# THE MILKY WAY

Phew! We made it. Now we've left the galaxy, we've been rewarded with this great view! Our galaxy is called the Milky Way and it's a beautiful spiral shape. The middle bulges with stars and at the centre is a supermassive black hole. Around 200 billion stars and their planets are held together in the galaxy by gravity.

This is where our Solar System sits. It's a tiny pinpoint in the galaxy, and looking back at it makes me feel very, very small!

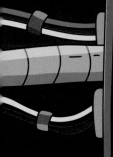

## MILKY WAY STATS

**LOCATION:** MILKY WAY GALAXY

**AGE:** 12–13 BILLION YEARS

**WIDTH:** 120,000 LIGHT YEARS

**ROTATION PERIOD:** 250 MILLION EARTH YEARS

**STARS WITHIN:** MORE THAN 200 BILLION

**MAJOR ARM NAMES:** PERSEUS, SAGITTARIUS, NORMA, SCUTUM-CENTAURUS, ORION SPUR

The Milky Way is just one of hundreds of billions of galaxies that exist in the universe. My brain can't even imagine how many stars that amounts to!

There are three main types of galaxy. The Milky Way is a spiral galaxy where new stars are generally formed in the outer arms.

Elliptical galaxies contain older stars in an organized shape. From a distance, they look like a hazy light.

Irregular galaxies are typically smaller. Their gravity is too weak to pull things into a spiral or ellipse, so they can look quite messy.

The shape of a galaxy is determined by its rotation speed, its mass and its age.

# COLLIDING GALAXIES

Behold 'The Mice'... a pair of colliding galaxies. Located 300 million light years from Earth, this duo are in the process of merging into one single giant galaxy. The wispy 'mice' tails are stars and gas thrown out during the collision.

Uh oh, that looks dangerous! Won't there be a huge explosion once they fully collide?

## COLLIDING GALAXY STATS

**LOCATION:** NGC4676 'THE MICE' COLLIDING GALAXIES, 290 MILLION LIGHT YEARS AWAY

**TIME FOR GALAXIES TO MERGE:** MILLIONS OF YEARS

**GALAXY SHAPES:** START SPIRAL, WILL END UP ELLIPTICAL

**STAR FORMATION RATE IN MERGING GALAXIES:** TEN TIMES ITS NORMAL PACE

Don't worry! It's just the galaxies' dust and gas clouds that merge. The result of this is lots of glittering newborn stars. This is what's happening here, in the Antennae galaxies collision.

It is a galaxy's gravity that attracts other nearby galaxies towards it. They pull each other closer over time. But as galaxies themselves are huge, the stars are just tiny dots within them. It's like grains of sand at opposite ends of a football field. So when it comes to collision time, most stars will actually miss each other.

In four billion years, the Milky Way and Andromeda galaxies may collide. They'll create 'Milkdromeda'!

# HEADING HOME

We've seen many beautiful sights in the universe, but there's nothing quite like home. It's time to head back and breathe in some fresh air again! But first we've got to survive one of our most challenging and dangerous missions ever: re-entry to Earth.

We've been travelling across space at warp speed, and as we approach Earth, gravity also starts to pull us down to the surface. If we keep going at this rate, we'll crash into the ground within seconds. Luckily, air molecules in the atmosphere rub against the space mobile causing friction and creating drag, which slows everything down. Unfortunately this also creates intense heat...

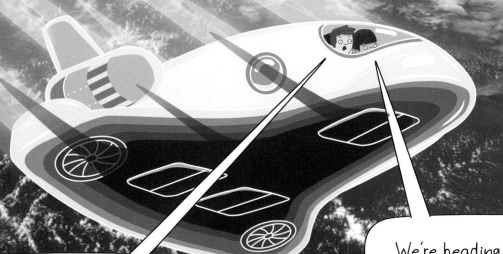

Our heat shields will protect us against these extreme temperatures, so we don't burn-up like a meteor.

We're heading for the ocean to cushion our landing. But a water impact could still damage the space mobile.

## RE-ENTRY STATS

LOCATION: EARTH'S ATMOSPHERE

RE-ENTRY BEGINS AT: 100 KM
(60 MI) ABOVE THE SURFACE

RE-ENTRY TEMPERATURE: 1,650°C (3,000°F)

PARACHUTES DEPLOYED AT:
3,200 M (10,500 FT)

RE-ENTRY DURATION:
APPROX. 14 MINUTES

Parachutes slow us down to just 20 kph (12.5 mph). We don't want to crash after all we've survived in space!

I can see the sea! Put the space mobile in sea mode for splashdown!

Hello Earth. Good to see you again.

# GLOSSARY

**Atmosphere**    The layer of gases that surrounds the Earth (and some other celestial bodies).

**Carbon dioxide**    A gas present in the atmosphere of Earth – and some other celestial bodies, including Venus – which traps the Sun's heat, raising temperatures.

**Constellation**    A group of stars arranged in a pattern, often named after how they look or a mythological creature.

**Crater**    A large hollow in the ground caused by the impact of a meteorite.

**Equator**    An imaginary line drawn around the centre of a planet or body that divides it into northern and southern hemispheres.

**Flyby**    When a spacecraft flies past a planet, or other body, but does not go into orbit or touch down on the surface.

**Friction**    A force that slows down two objects moving over each other.

**Galaxy**    A group of millions of stars and their orbiting planetary systems, plus gas and dust, all held together by gravity.

**Gamma rays**    High-energy waves that can't be seen by the human eye.

**Geyser**    A hot spring in the ground that sends out a tall column of liquid and steam into the air.

**Gravity**    The force that attracts two bodies towards each other. The greater the mass, the greater the pull of gravity.

**Light year**    The distance that light travels in one Earth year – around 9 trillion km (6 trillion mi).

**Magma**    Hot, molten rock under the surface of Earth or another celestial body.

**Mass**    The amount of material an object has, which on Earth also indicates how heavy it is.

**Methane**    A chemical compound which is usually a gas on Earth, but which can be a liquid or a solid in the freezing temperatures of the outer Solar System.

| | |
|---|---|
| NASA | The National Aeronautics and Space Administration agency of the USA. It is the agency in charge of US space exploration. |
| Nuclear fusion | A process where atoms are pushed together to release huge amounts of energy. |
| Orbit | The curved path of an object around a star, planet or moon. |
| Orbiter | A spacecraft that goes into orbit – flying repeatedly around – a body. |
| Oxygen | A gas that is essential for animal life to occur. |
| Rover | A space vehicle that explores the surface of a planet or other body. |
| Sedimentary rock | A type of rock formed when fragments of other rock – often created by the action of flowing water – are deposited on top of each other in layers. |
| Solar panel | A panel that absorbs the Sun's light and turns it into electricity. |
| Solar System | The planets, moons and other smaller bodies that orbit the Sun or another star. |
| Spectrometer | A scientific instrument that measures light wavelengths. |
| Supernova | The explosion of a large star. |
| Ultraviolet | High-energy waves with a wavelength that means they sit just beyond the spectrum of light waves that humans can see. |
| Vacuum | Space that is empty of all matter. |
| X-ray | High-energy waves that can pass through many solid objects that visible light cannot. |

# PICTURE CREDITS

STAY IN TOUCH – lonelyplanet.com/contact

Lonely Planet Offices:

AUSTRALIA the Malt Store, Level 3, 551 Swanston St, Carlton,
Victoria 3053 T: 03 8379 8000

IRELAND Digital Depot, Roe Lane (off Thomas St),
Digital Hub, Dublin 8, D08 TCV4, Ireland

USA 124 Linden St, Oakland, CA 94607 T: 510 250 6400

UK 240 Blackfriars Rd, London, SE1 8NW T: 020 3771 5100